BASS-ICK THEORY
Music theory and life lessons for bassists

By Tony Muhammad

© Tony Muhammad 2020, San Diego, California

Copyright 2020 Tony Muhammad.
All rights reserved. No part of this book may be used or reproduced in any manner without written permission from the author.

https://www.facebook.com/tony.muhammad.33

Introduction

This book is written especially for bass players. As a bass player, it is necessary to learn, understand, and memorize some basic theory. One of my intentions when I thought to create the **BASS-ICK THEORY** book was to have it feel like whoever is reading this is actually present with me and we are having a conversation about music - playing bass to be more specific. So, if that's the case let's start by looking at the definition of theory:

THEORY – A coherent group of tested general propositions regarded as correct that can be used as principles of explanations and prediction.

If you are not familiar with some amount of theory, it will be almost impossible to effectively execute your job as a bassist and you will have difficulty communicating with musicians that are able to speak the language. I was taught bass by the late great legendary jazz bassist Milt "Judge" Hinton. I can still hear his raspy voice and see his hand motions as he would tell me, "You have to do your job." Milt also used to yell at me on occasion, saying, "No, no, no, Tony, you got to identify the chord!" In everything he did and said, Milt helped me become a better bassist. I sincerely hope the information in this book will help you become a better bassist. As you will soon see, you won't find notes written on the musical staff in this first volume of **BASS-ICK THEORY.** That way, any bassist that has not yet learned to read music will still be able to obtain some information from this book. Even though there is a lot of information in the book, it will just barely scratch the surface of the direction that you might want to head. I will also share some of the learning experiences that came my way, in hopes that they may assist you in becoming a better bassist, too. Moving forward in the next volume of **BASS-ICK THEORY**, you will see notes and musical notation. Being able to read music will open more opportunities for you as a bassist. Throughout the book you will also notice many quotes. The quotes are from my favorite bassists, who also happen to be outstanding human beings. All of the quotes will

The author with Milt "Judge" Hinton

"Don't be sharp, don't be flat, just be natural"

—Milt Hinton

help you in one way or another, although some are inside stories and jokes. These bassists have been doing what they do for years and they were kind enough to share some of the wisdom they've gathered over those years. Some quotes might make you laugh, while others will make you sit back and think. Now that I think of it, just about all of the bass players I know have a huge sense of humor. And now might also be a good time to mention that, if you see a quote from Leroy, you should know that Leroy is a fictional character - although we all know Leroy. He's the guy that's late for the gig. The guy that you might just smell the odor of an alcoholic beverage on his breath. He's the guy that will show up without a ¼ inch cord to plug into the amp. Leroy's the guy that might wear the wrong color shirt on the gig. He's the guy that will show up at the airport a day early because he misread the itinerary. Leroy's the guy that, once he gets there, he can flat out just play. He can get it in with the best of them. And I am not 100% sure, but Leroy can probably play bass and some keys too.

There are fifteen exercises suggested in this book. I truly believe that if you are a beginner and just learning to play, they will help you form a solid foundation. And if you can already find your way around the bass, you will still find a lot that can help you grow and develop your skills and understanding as a bassist. If you are new to learning bass, use this book along with someone who understands basic theory and that should be enough to help you get to it. Take your time and go through each exercise thoroughly to get the most out of it.

On another note, the idea for the cover of this book came after thinking of all of my favorite bass players. In most books the cover sets the tone for what's ahead. Take another look at the cover of this book. I carefully selected Bass players that I truly respect for who they are, what they have done and what they are still doing. If your name is there, thank you for what you do.

"It's about time.....
I think it's a great idea to pay homage to all the Bass heroes out there, especially the unknown."
—Dennis Chambers

Our beloved friend and fellow bassist
Vince Loving
Rest in peace, Brother

"Music is a gift. Music is healing. Music brings humanity together as one. Music is the universal language of peace and love."   —Jimmy Haslip

"The bass is to music as the sun is to the planets; it serves as the gravitational center of a system around which all involved orbit as they do their own thing."   —Tony Bunn

"The atmosphere in the courtyard of the Goethe-Institute compound in Dar es Salaam was loose and casual, the attendees to the workshop only a few. As I sat there listening to the bassist's approach to their own music, trying to find a bridge between their culture and mine, an idea for a really simple exercise suddenly crystalized: Pick a pattern of any length and play it without deviation or embellishment for as long as possible. After about three – five minutes, the difficulty of this exercise became evident to us all. But when the bassist continued the exercise for longer periods, some for up to a half hour, something quite magical began to occur. People who weren't involved in the workshop and before had no interest in our gathering when we were just noodling around, all of a sudden began to hover – drawn in by the low-frequency mantras wafting through the air. As the process continued, certain individuals would come, stop and then go, again and again. It was almost as if their silent orbits formed a part of a larger music whose gravity derived from the endlessly repetitive bass patterns. When we stopped this exercise, so too did the noticeable cycling of others through our space."

—Tony Bunn

"Music is oxygen for the soul."
—Nathan Brown

"Music is not what I do, it's who I am."
—Michael Kennedy

This book is dedicated to
"Lil man"
Miles Monroe Eugene Boganey

"Learn the basics, learn to read music, love every note."
— Jessie Powers

And now, it's time to learn some **BASS-ICK THEORY**.
We'll start with a concept that bassists use in every piece of music.

Intervals

An interval is the space between any two notes. All intervals should be memorized visually and by ear. Please memorize the intervals below, listed from smallest to largest. I decided to use the letter A as my starting point, because of the natural half step between B & C, and E & F.

A to B flat	can be called a minor 2nd, half step, or semi tone
A to B	can be called a Major 2nd or whole step
A to C	can be called a minor 3rd, or whole step & half step
A to C#	can be called a Major third or 2 whole steps
A to D	can be called a perfect 4th
A to D#	raised 4th
A to E flat	lowered 5th
A to E	perfect 5th
A to F	minor 6th
A to F#	Major 6th
A to G	minor 7th
A to G#	Major 7th
A to A	perfect octave

"One of the most important things you can do as a musician is to listen...you might just learn something."

-Al Turner

Intervals are very important to learn and recognize. A very good way to learn them is by finding a song, jingle, nursery rhyme or any sound that you hear frequently that contains each interval. Find your own unique way of learning to hear and identify these sounds when you hear them. What interval do you hear when your doorbell rings? What about the sounds you hear when you start your vehicle? Be curious about any sound that you hear. What intervals do the emergency vehicles use? Why do they use those particular sounds? What sounds are played in movies when something bad is about to happen? What sound is played when the great white shark, Jaws, is about to get lunch? What intervals do you hear when Michael Myers in the movie Halloween slowly walks down toward whoever he's about to handle? Once you get started, your ears will soon grow bigger. If you find sounds that you're used to hearing that reflect each interval, it will be easier for you to learn and remember them. After choosing an interval that you recognize, you can then learn what the first note is. That will also help you with your pitch recognition because whenever you hear that exact note, you will automatically know what note you are hearing. Most of us don't have perfect pitch - we have relative pitch - and we can improve this by using this exercise.

You should be able to sing any interval on demand. Depending on how old you are, you might remember the three tones that were played each time the station NBC announced itself. When I heard it, I was curious to know what those sounds were and later I learned it was 1 then 6 then 4. When I watched the Wizard of Oz, I heard the song Somewhere Over the Rainbow and learned that the first two notes were octaves then a major seven. When I watched the scene of the little soldiers marching in the castle and singing, Ohh – EEE – Ohh – OOO – OOO. I found out it was 1 - 5 – 1 – 5 - 1. Whenever I went for a ride in my father's car, whatever song that came on the radio I tried to play it on my flute. I might have been really getting on my father's nerves, but he never said anything or told me to shut up. He just drove and continued to listen to the horrible flute music I was providing.

"If we play the root, we determine the chord."

—Mark Russell

As you practice connecting intervals, you will then learn to build chords. Start on any given note and build seconds, thirds, fourths etc.

Chords

Chords are built by connecting two or more intervals. The chords you will use most commonly are the major and minor chords. Some theory experts say that there are 86 different types of chords. We will talk about the ones you will use most often.

Major chord- a basic major chord consists of three notes. The bottom note we can call the root. The second or middle note is called the third, and the top note is called the fifth. If you play the notes of a chord one note at a time it can be called an arpeggio. The major chord is constructed by creating the following intervals:

$$\text{Root} \rightarrow \text{Major } 3^{rd} \rightarrow \text{minor } 3^{rd}$$

You will see that the minor 3rd at the end of the chord is the 5th of the root you played as the first note in the chord.

Minor chord – a basic minor chord also consists of three notes: the root, 3rd and 5th. However, the minor chord is constructed by creating the following intervals:

$$\text{Root} \rightarrow \text{minor } 3^{rd} \rightarrow \text{Major } 3^{rd}$$

Again, you will see that the Major 3rd at the end of the chord is the 5th of the root you played as the first note in the chord.

"If you don't know the chord, you don't know the tune."
— Gary Grainger

A Major   A C# E
Check the intervals: from A to C# is a Major 3rd, From C# to E is a minor 3rd and from A to E is a perfect 5th.

A minor   A C E
Check the intervals: from A to C is a minor 3rd, from C to E is a Major third, and from A to E is a perfect 5th.

Then, there are other chords that are created by using different intervals. Once you know what intervals are used to create each type of chord, you will easily be able to play them anywhere on your bass.

A diminished   A C E flat
Check the intervals: from A to C is a minor 3rd. from C to E flat is also a minor 3rd.
        Root → minor 3rd → minor 3rd

A Augmented   A C# E# (F)
Check the intervals: from A to C# is a Major 3rd and from C# to E# is a Major 3rd.
        Root → Major 3rd → Major 3rd

A Sus4   A D E
Check the intervals: from A to D is a perfect 4th and from D to E is a Major 2nd. From A to E is a perfect 5th.
        Root → perfect 4th → Major 2nd

A sus2   A B E
Check the intervals: from A to B is a Major 2nd and from B to E is a perfect 4th. A to E is a perfect 5th.
        Root → Major 2nd → perfect 4th

"Be a Musician, don't just talk about music."
 —Dennis Chambers

Seventh Chords

A seventh chord has at least four notes in it. The reason it's called a seventh chord is because the interval from the root of the chord to the seventh of the chord is either a major or minor 7th.

Example: A Major 7th A C# E G#
Check the intervals: from A to C# is a Major 3rd, from C# to E is a minor 3rd, from E to G# is a Major third, from A to G# is a Major seventh.
         Root → Major 3rd → minor 3rd → Major 3rd

Example: A minor 7th A C E G
Check the intervals: from A to C is a minor 3rd, from C to E is a Major 3rd, from E to G is a minor 3rd, from A to G is a minor seventh.
         Root → minor 3rd → Major 3rd → minor 3rd

Example: A minor 7th flat 5   A C E flat G (sometimes called a half diminished chord)
Check the intervals: from A to C is a minor third, from C to E flat is a minor third, and from E flat to G is a Major third.

         Root → minor 3rd → minor 3rd → Major 3rd

Example: A diminished 7th A C E flat G flat
Check the intervals: from A to C is a minor 3rd, from C to E flat is a minor 3rd and from E flat to G flat is a minor third.

         Root → minor 3rd → minor 3rd → minor 3rd

Example: A Dominant 7th A   C#   E   G
Check the intervals: from A to C# is a Major 3rd, from C# to E is a minor 3rd, from E to G is a minor 3rd.

         Root → Major 3rd → minor 3rd → minor 3rd

"When it comes to musical growth, the more comfortable you are outside of your comfort zone the better."
　　　　　　　　　　　　　　－Harley Magsino

Inversions

Inversions of a chord simply are created by starting on a different note than the root. Depending on how many notes there are in a chord will determine what inversions are available to you. A three note chord would have two possible inversions in addition to the root, or original, position. The first inversion would position the third as the new root of the chord, the fifth would become the third, and the original root would be on top of the chord. The second inversion would be created by first playing the fifth as the bottom of the chord, followed by the original root and finally the original third as the top of the chord.

The root position would be played: root - 3rd - 5th
The first inversion would be played: 3rd - 5th - root
The third inversion would be played: 5th – root - 3rd

You will create inversions in the same way for a seventh chord.
The root position would be played: root – 3rd – 5th – 7th
The first inversion would be played: 3rd – 5th – 7th – root
The second inversion would be played: 5th – 7th – root – 3rd
The third inversion would be played: 7th – root – 3rd -5th
You will get an idea of how inversions can be helpful to you when we get to the section on learning new tunes.

Scales

Scales are created by connecting a series of intervals, mostly Major and minor seconds, and sometimes a minor 3rd. The first scale we should look at is called the chromatic scale. It is built by starting on the root and consecutively building minor seconds.

Chromatic A A# B C C# D D# E F F# G G# A

            A Bb B C Db D Eb E F Gb G Ab A

"How you do anything is how you do everything. Whenever we practice anything, we are practicing playing music. Always make sure to play with good feel, tone and articulation. Never just blast through an exercise sloppily. You are then only reinforcing sloppy playing. Put everything you've got into everything you play."
                              —Damian Erskine

When you practice the chromatic or any scale, make sure you keep good time and that you aim to have all the notes sound warm, round, and connected.

Major Scale: A B C# D E F# G# A   *Chord:* A C# E G#

The Major scale is constructed of whole steps and half steps. Check the intervals and you will notice a half step between the 3rd & 4th notes and between the 7th and 8th notes. Always remember that there is naturally a half step between B & C and between E & F. A very good way to learn your major scales is to pick any note and remember whole steps until 3 and 4 then again at 7 and 8. The sequence of whole and half notes is:

whole – whole – half – whole – whole – whole – half

If you don't land on the root note an octave higher after the seventh note, then you need to figure out where you dropped the ball.

The Major chord comes directly from the Major scale. Start at the root and skip every other note to build the major 7th chord.

If we rewrite the Major scale starting on the second note instead of the first note, we will build another scale. There is a specific name for this new scale, but for now we can call it a **TWO scale**.

Scale: B C# D E F# G# A B   *Chord:* B D F# A

Carefully check the intervals, as the naturally formed half steps have shifted. The sequence of whole and half notes for this new scale is:

whole – half – whole - whole – whole – half – whole

If you start on the root of this scale and skip every other note you will build a different type of chord. The chord that is formed is a minor chord. There are several types of minor chords, but to be more specific for now we can call this a TWO chord, just like we are calling this a TWO scale. When learning music theory, you will have to learn many new words and names because you are learning a new language, but with time, they will become very natural for you.

"If you heard something, you might just hear something."

—Leroy

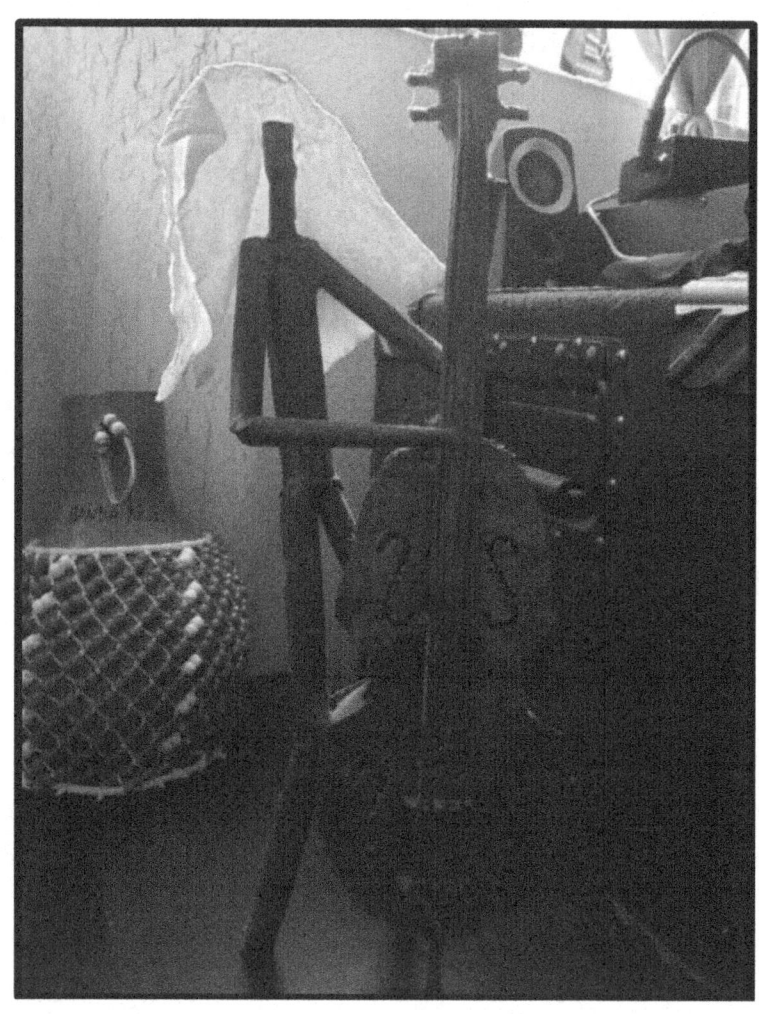

Scale: C# D E F# G# A B C#   *Chord:* C# E G# B

This is the same scale, rewritten starting on the third note so you can call it a **THREE scale**. You will notice that, once again, the half steps have shifted. The sequence of whole and half notes for this new scale is:

        half – whole – whole - whole – half – whole – whole

And if you skip every other note in this scale you will have another minor type chord. You can call this chord a THREE chord for now.

Scale: D E F# G# A B C# D   *Chord:* D F# A C#

This is the same scale rewritten starting from the fourth note so you can call is a **FOUR scale**. If you start from the root note of this scale and skip every other note you will build a major chord, which you can call a FOUR chord. As with each of these rewritten scales, the half steps continue to shift and present different opportunities for the chords that can be constructed. The sequence of whole and half notes for this new scale is:

        whole – whole – whole - half – whole – whole – half

In this scale particularly, the first half step falls between the 4th and 5th note. If we want to make use of that naturally formed half step, we can add that note to our Major chord and build a very nice sounding chord. It would still be a Major chord, but the fourth note is a half step higher, or sharp, compared with our original Major scale. When we add the 4th note to our Major chord it would look like this: D F# A C# G#

This new chord would be called D Major 7 # 11. In this chord, the fourth note of the scale is sharp, compared to the original Major scale and the #11 is the 4th note one octave higher.

Scale: E F# G# A B C# D E   *Chord:* E G# B D

This is our same scale rewritten from the fifth note, which you can call the **FIVE scale**. If we start on the new root and skip every other note once again, we can build a very strong sounding chord, hence the name **DOMINANT CHORD**. The dominant

"Knowledge not used skillfully is a testament to your true understanding."

—Leroy

"Anyone can hear the music. Takes someone special to Feel the Bass. (C U in the funny book) God bless"

—Tony Banda

chord is used in most music because of its strong presence. You can call this a FIVE scale and a FIVE chord if you like. The sequence of whole and half notes for this new scale is:
    whole – whole – half - whole – whole – half – whole

Scale: F# G# A B C# D E F#   *Chord:* F# A C# E

This is the scale rewritten from the sixth note. When we start at the root of this scale and skip every other note, we will build another minor type chord. We can call the scale a **SIX scale** and the chord a SIX chord. The sequence of whole and half notes for this new scale is:
    whole – half – whole - whole – half – whole – whole

Scale: G# A B C# D E F# G#   *Chord:* G# B D F#

This is the scale rewritten from the 7th and final note before you arrive back at the root. You could call it a **SEVEN scale**. If you start on the root and skip every other note you will build a minor chord. This minor chord is a little bit different and has a different sound than the other minor chords we have seen so far. Check the intervals and you will notice that, due to the half steps continuing to shift, the fifth of this minor chord is lowered. This chord is called a minor 7th Flat 5 or a half diminished chord. The sequence of whole and half notes for this new scale is:
    half – whole – whole - half – whole – whole – whole

There are several ways to practice scales that will help you learn them and how to use them anywhere on your bass. Once you decide on the scale you want to practice, try starting below the root note of that scale. Eventually, you should start the intended scale on the lowest note from the scale on your bass. An example would be if you wanted to practice a C major scale and you are playing a four string bass, try starting that scale with the open E. that's the lowest note on your bass. That would mean playing E F G A B and then the C major scale. Play the scale past the root up to the nine, which is the octave of the two. The nine will have a decent tone that will be a very good place to turn the

"A good friend of mine who wasn't the sharpest knife in the drawer (Leroy's cousin), was a big music fan, a great salsa dancer, and all around cool dude. He used to complement the band when he felt it swinging by saying, "If it ain't swing, it don't mean a thing." I'm sure you know what he was trying to say!!!!"
Do wop do wap do wap do wap do wap do wap do wap do waaa!!!

—Ruben Rodriguez

scale around and return to the starting point. After you are comfortable with this, continue past the nine to the highest note on your bass that is in the scale. Many musicians only play the scale from the first note to the octave and then return to the starting point, but by doing that, your ears will not get used to the extensions above and below the scale. And when you start out, always use a metronome or drum machine to help you keep the forward swinging feeling.

Tetra chords – Another good way to practice your scales would be through the use of tetra chords. A tetra chord is four notes. Most of the scales that you use will have eight notes. The tetra chord would be the first four notes. If you divide the major scale into two sections that would show you the two tetra chords. They will be separated by either a half step or a whole step. For example, the scale beginning on A would be divided like this:

A B C# D - E F#G# A - these are both called # 1 tetra chord.

Notice the intervals between each #1 tetrachord - they are identical and are made by a whole step followed by another whole step and then a half step. We can say this is a number one tetra chord.

If you build tetra chords starting from the second note of that same scale you will see that this tetrachord is made by a whole step followed by a half step and then a whole step.

B C# D E – F# G# A B - this can be called #2 tetrachord

Check out the intervals and see where the half steps fall when you start the tetrachords on the third note of the scale. Since the half steps shift, this creates a different tetrachord.

C# D E F#- G# A B C - this can be called #3 tetrachord

D E F# G#- A B C# D – this is a #4 tetrachord followed by a #1 tetrachord.

Carefully check out the intervals. Notice the # 4 tetrachord is whole steps only. Continue writing out this scale so you are able to notice how the pattern continues. You will easily be able to use tetrachords in your playing once you learn them.

Exercise # 1 Practice playing your scales starting on the lowest note in that scale on your bass. Play first up to the nine, and then as high as you are comfortable. When you feel comfortable, try descending the scale.

Exercise # 2 Diatonic thirds Practice the scales using diatonic thirds. The word diatonic refers to within the key. Play the root, then skip over the second note and play the third note. Continue playing the next note and skipping the following note. When you play every other note, you are creating thirds. The thirds you are creating are either major or minor. Check your intervals or fingering to determine whether you are playing minor or major thirds.

As mentioned, it is perfectly ok to call these scales by their numbered names. You might also hear them referred to as **modes**. You can make it a personal project to learn the names at your convenience. I often create what I call "bass projects," which are things I want to learn that take some time to really understand or become comfortable with. Projects might be anything from learning a new melody or attempting to create an arrangement for how to best present a new tune to the band. Creating projects for yourself will help you make better sense of the time you decide to practice. With a project, you have an intended purpose for your practice session.
The modes that we used numbers for earlier can also be referred to by these names:

1. Ionian
2. Dorian
3. Phrygian
4. Lydian

5. Mixolydian
6. Aeolian
7. Locrian

Here are a few other scales that you will want to learn with time. These scales can be checked out later, but for right now, the major scale and its modes are a good starting point. It might be a good idea to bite off a small chunk at a time.

Melodic minor scale
Harmonic minor scale
Blues scale
Diminished scale
Pentatonic scale

Each of these scales can also be rewritten starting on different notes. Because of the shifting half steps, they will create different chords that would be nice to add to your library of chords. The bass player should be a walking dictionary of chords and scales. Both the Melodic minor scale and the Harmonic minor scale will teach several new and very distinct chords. Once you are comfortable with the basic scales, there's a book written by **Jimmy Haslip** with a library of different melodic scales that would be an excellent book to add to your library.

"Look at the fingerboard and music like the universe or a galaxy unexplored, unknown, anywhere."
                                   -Lonnie Plaxico

Circle of fourths – The circle of fourths is just that - a circle made of notes that are each a perfect fourth higher or lower than the notes on either side of it. There are twelve notes, and after that, they repeat themselves again an octave higher or lower depending on which way you travel. The circle of 4ths can be a great way to practice everything you have learned. By using the circle of fourths, you will play every key signature. If you move in the opposite direction, a perfect fourth becomes a perfect fifth. Normally I like to use a clock-like diagram as you see below. I will start with C this time because the key of C does not have any sharps or flats. The sharps and flats gradually increase by one each time, depending on the direction you start. (The key of F has one flat, the key of Bb has two flats, etc. The key of G has one sharp, the key of D has two sharps, etc.) The bass is set up using perfect 4ths. Each time you move across the neck to the very next note or string you are moving in perfect fourths. Bass players should know perfect fourths easily.

C   F   Bb   Eb   Ab   Db   Gb   Cb   E   A   D   G   C

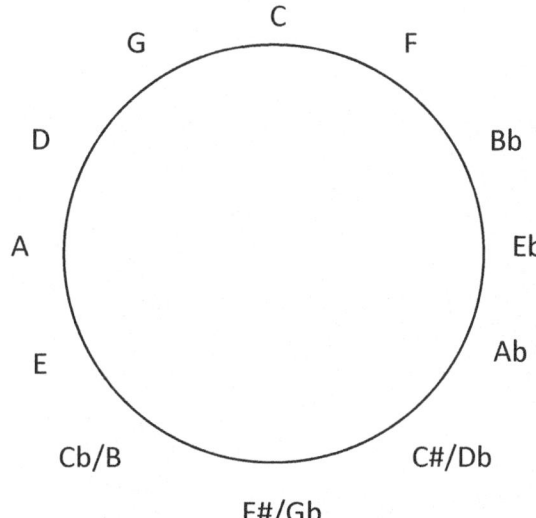

"I thought you had said wear a purple suit and purple hat. Ohhh, my bad."
—Leroy

Exercise # 3 Practice all 12 Major scales using the circle of fourths. Continue from one scale to the next without losing time. Practice each mode around the circle of fourths also.

It would be an excellent idea to practice the chords and scales moving first in perfect fourths and then perfect fifths. As I mentioned earlier, if you are learning to play jazz, using a drum beat that's swinging would be helpful. Otherwise, a metronome would do the job just as well. Start with a comfortable tempo and increase when possible.

The job of the bass player

Milt would always tell me that you have to "do your job." But what is the job of a bass player? I can tell you that it's a lot more than knowing the theory in this book. As you progress forward in your musical endeavors you will come across many different issues, attitudes, egos, etc. Lots of time, the issues you deal with will not even be related to music at all. You might run into very talented musicians that have never studied music at all. There are many fantastic musicians that have never studied one bit of theory in their lifetime. Some of these musicians can still get the job done. To be able to play any instrument is a blessing and a spiritual gift. Studying some music theory can be a big help in your quest to becoming a better musician. The end goal is to be able to effectively communicate with your fellow musicians. One item that should be high up on the list is to **"BE KIND"** during the process. There are countless situations where a musician might be a phenomenal player but is not a very nice person. What they might notice is that, although they are a great player, they never get the opportunity to play with certain musicians again, because of their very unpleasant attitude.

"Bass grooves have gotta be thick and juicy, and sometimes you have to slap it to get things to jiggle."
        —Rene Camacho

For the most part, the job of the bassist is to find a unique way to define, outline, and connect the chords of a tune and create a smoothly flowing bass line that holds everything together. Another job of the bass player is to "keep the groove." Basically, we lay it down. Sometimes I like to refer to the bass player as the "base" player. There are many outstanding bass players that have mastered this task. They make it look and sound easy. I have a very good friend and fellow bassist out of New York whose name is **Bill Dotts**. Bill can lay down a groove so hard that you can watch a clock tick to his groove. His intensity is such that while he is playing his groove you can see sweat drip from his hands from time to time. I am not joking. Another excellent example would be **Rodney "Skeet" Curtis**. Skeet has been playing funky grooves for decades. He can lay down a groove so funky that it will make you dance, smile, and crack jokes at the same time. Skeet could probably tell you an extremely funny joke at the same time that he's playing the groove. Then there's **Eddie Resto**. Eddie is a master at playing many types of Latin music. Don't be surprised if you have a hard time trying to decide whether you want to dance or just listen to the bass line. It will be hard to do both. Eddie commonly refers to what he does as "dropping bombs," or sometimes refers to it as "RONK." I could go on and on, but the point is to check some or all of these cats out. A good bass player is a stable person who anchors the music down so the other musicians can feel free to improvise on top of it. The bass player should know the melody and the chords to every song and should learn to play in as many styles as possible. The bass player also needs to be able to recognize the downbeat and all time signatures.

Exercise # 4 | B -7 | E7 |

If you are a jazz bassist, you will see this one time and time again in every key possible. This is the 2-5 progression. Take as much time as possible working on this. Start out by outlining these two chords. Learn to spell each chord while playing with a metronome or drum machine. Start out at a very slow swinging tempo. When you are comfortable moving between these two chords, try inserting a non-chord tone either a half step above or below your upcoming target. These could be called either passing tones or upper or lower neighbors. Being able to spell these chords while keeping a steady time will be a good foundation for you to use to learn to walk through chord changes. As an added suggestion, after you are sort of comfortable spelling the B-7 chord try *F# A C# E* over top of the B-7 to see if your ears are ok with the way this sounds over the chord. Also, try playing *F Ab C E G* over the E 7 chord. If you like it, examine the relationship of these notes and how they relate to the chord. Keep in mind that one of the main functions of your job as a jazz bassist is to keep a nice swinging feel to your bass line.

Diatonic chord movement

Diatonic means within the key. Once you have learned to recognize all intervals when you see them, you can use this to your advantage when you are creating your walking bass lines. When you see chords diatonically moving either a Major or minor second, you will find that these two chords have one note in common between the two of them.
For example, C Major 7 *C E G B* moving to a D minor 7 *D F A C* will only have the note C in common.

With diatonic chord movement that moves a third, the chords will have three notes in common.
For example, C Major 7 *C E G B* moving to an E minor 7 *E G B D* have the E, G and B in common.

Diatonic chord movement that moves a 5th or 4th will have two common notes.
For example, C Major 7 *C E G B* moving to G Dominant 7 *G B D F* or C Major 7 *C E G B* moving to F Major 7 *F A C E*.

This is the good stuff to keep in mind when you are walking through chord changes.

Let's take a look at a commonly seen four note chord progression. This progression is used in many ways in the music we listen to, whether it's played as a vamp at the end of the set, as an intro piece, or even as a groove in a reggae tune. Sometimes a band member might say 1 6 2 5 in B flat and then once the groove starts, he might make an announcement to the listeners, mentioning we'll be right back or don't forget to tip your waitress, etc. We are going to continue to use the key of A major.

This chord progression has two chords per measure.

Exercise # 5 | A Maj 7   F# -7 | B -7   E 7 |

It might be a good idea to select a nice pattern on your drum machine or the rhythm section of the iRealPro to a very slow tempo. Remove the bass and the keyboard from the track. If by this time you have not committed the notes of each chord to memory, write them down so you can see each note. This progression is written with two chords per measure. The first approach again should be to spell each chord note by note. As you spell or arpeggiate the chords, hear what you play. Relax to your sound. Keep the tones big, warm, round, and connected. Always study yourself. Since you don't have keyboard in the mix there is no rush to get to the next chord. Try inserting non chord tones between the chord tones. When I play over minor chords, I sometimes play the root, followed by the two which is a non-chord tone, and then after the two, I play the 3rd. It gives it a bit

"Every musical thought you produce should have your signature on it."
        —Leroy

"The best way to lose a gig is running your mouth all the time."
        —Cecil McBee, Jr.

of a forward motion movement. Sometimes when starting on a major chord I play the 3rd of the chord on beat one. Sometimes when playing over a dominant chord I might start with the root an octave up, then play the 7th. In this case that would be E, D, and then if you play the 3rd of A major that would be C#. That would give you a downward motion.

Stay mindful when it comes to the direction of movement of your bass line. If you study the notes of each chord in the progression you can find interesting ways to connect the chords. Listen to bass players like Ron Carter. Ron is a master at building walking bass lines. Again, take a very small bite. Start by taking one chord at a time until you have internalized the note choices well enough to use them on command and over any chord.

Many times when playing a jazz standard, during the melody the bass player will play what's called a two feel. A two feel is played by playing mostly half notes with a whole note here and there. The two feel supports the tune and does not interfere with the melody. I have learned that a jazz bassist who has a solid feel with a big strong tone and is able to walk through the changes and take a decent solo here and there is always welcomed on a gig. You don't have to be the biggest or fanciest cat in town. Just get the job done and move on to the next gig.

All bass players are not going to be readers. If you have a good understanding of the chords and how they work in conjunction with the melody, you will be ok, but it would be better for you to actually learn to read.
I know quite a few bassists who lose gigs or don't accept gigs because the gig requires some reading. With the melody, you will be able to get your job done. But it would be better if you would invest the time to actually learn to read.

"A good bass line isn't about how many notes you play. It's about the impact the notes you play have on the music."
                                                          —Irvin Madden

"Playing bass is like driving a car. Stay in your lane."   —Butch Coleman

Feel

It may be rather difficult to teach a bassist how to play with a good feel. You can learn to play with a good feel by listening to good examples set by master bassists. Some musicians are born with a natural feel. Some have to develop a good feel over time. To me, music is a conversation that can go in many different directions. Think about the last time you had a good conversation with two or more people present. There was most likely a decent balance between everyone involved. Maybe one person was sharing his or her story, and while the story was being shared, you listened. Hopefully, your body language during the story acknowledged that you were listening. Every now and then you might comment. When you are playing music, it should be the same way. Sometimes people go on and on with a long drawn out saga, and this happens in music too. Some people just flat out talk entirely too much. Sometimes people are rude and talk over you or cut you off while you are speaking. Some people don't listen well, or just don't listen at all. Well guess what, all these things plus more happen in music also. I have many good friends, but this particular friend of mine stands out as I am bringing up this point. This friend, who shall remain nameless (*Anthony Payne*), whenever he would miss a cue or error, which was hardly ever, he had the perfect response. After it was brought to his attention he would simply say, "You'll have this in life," and then he would move right on to the next thing as if it never happened. The more you listen to the musical conversation that the musicians are having, the better you can understand the point being made and this will allow you to contribute to the conversation more effectively. I believe music is very spiritual, especially the bass and the drums. I also believe it is a gift to be blessed with the spirit of being able to create music. Many people listen to music, but not as many people can actually hear the music. Bass players are unique people and usually a bass player can immediately feel the results of what they have created. They can see how the bass line or groove affects people in a live situation. They can see if folks dance, move side to side or

"Music is the absence and playing of notes."
    -Ernest Abdul-Raheem

whatever else folks do when they hear a bass groove. The jazz bassist can tell if his line is swinging enough to get heads moving. Sometimes, a person that really loves jazz and knows how to listen might just look at you with a slight smile and give you a head nod. That's the sign of approval. Also, remember that you are playing for the audience and with your fellow musicians - not just for yourself.

Exercise # 6 | C -7 | F7 | Bb Maj 7| Eb Maj 7|
                    | A -7 b5 | D7 b13| G -6 | G -6 |

These are the first eight bars to Autumn Leaves

Just as before, take time to spell each of these chords individually. One of the chords has an altered/added note: the b13 in the D7 is the octave of the 6th, lowered a half step. The G-6 is self- explanatory. The bass player should know all chords. He/she should know how to spell every chord. The name of the chord actually explains what notes are needed to construct it. Try to get as comfortable as possible spelling these chord progressions.
Using the metronome or drum machine should help you stay on track. If you are able to lock with the time, it will be easier to start walking through the changes once you add a rhythm instrument to the mix.

We all will face interesting, meaningful and/or difficult situations in this life. One thought I had was that you may experience the same or a similar situation as I have. I hope that if I share an interesting, funny, or very educational experience with you, then maybe I can prevent you from having to go through a similar situation. We all are a total of everything that we have experienced during our lifetime. We all have to find our way, and sometimes with a little help from one another we can make it a little easier for each other by sharing.

"Can your brother do this?"
　　　　　　　　－Greg Grainger

I was born and raised in Baltimore, Maryland. I loved listening to music from as far back as I could remember. Baltimore has always been the home of many well known musicians. When I decided I wanted to seriously learn to play bass, just a few blocks away was bassist **Gary Grainger**. Gary was a few years older than I, but his younger brother, Greg, and I were the same age and went to school together. Greg made it possible for me to get to know Gary. Soon after, Gary moved about an hour away. One day I got in my mom's car and drove the hour to Gary's house for my first lesson. He asked me to play a blues. I played something, although I can't say it was a blues. Gary interrupted me and said, "What chords are you outlining?" I said, "What are you talking about?" That's when Gary said, "If you don't know the chord, you don't know the tune." I said, "Ok, what does that mean?" Gary again said, "If you don't know the chord, you don't know the tune." I said, "I heard what you said, but what does that mean?" Gary just repeated, "If you don't know the chord, you don't know the tune." I said, "Ok man, I don't want no bass lesson." Since Gary was older and bigger then I was, inside my head I also said, "!$#@%*&#." Then I got behind the wheel of my mother's car and drove back home in the rush hour traffic. Halfway home a light bulb went off in my head as to what, "If you don't know the chord, you don't know the tune" means. Today, 40 years later, Gary and I still laugh at that. This is a funny story now whenever I think to it. Back then it was everything but funny. You should learn from this and any other episode that follows. As my friend, the one that I said should remain unnamed (Anthony Payne) would say, **YOU WILL HAVE THIS IN LIFE.**

Exercise # 7 | F -7 |Bb7| F -7| Bb7|
     | F -7 |Bb7| F -7| C7#9|

These are the first 8 bars of a waltz written by Wes Montgomery called Full House.
A waltz is normally played in ¾ time signature, but you can also work on this progression in common (4/4) time.
I like to use this example because of the chord layout. Notice the F-7 chord (the two chord) continues to move to the Bb7 chord,

"My tone has helped me survive."
—Kevin Cooper

"How you touch your bass can be a big factor in developing your tone."
—Mark Russell

which is the five chord of the key. You will see this 2-5 progression many times in music. You can create a nice sequence on a progression like this. I remember hearing Herbie Hancock on a video say sequences sound best when played in groups of two, and a group of three should be the max. The above exercise is set up for a sequence of three, but I would play a sequence of two and use the third F-7 to Bb7 as a type of response.

Tone

Creating your tone is a very important aspect of being a well-rounded bassist. Milt used to say the bass tone should be BIG + FAT. He also said the notes should be warm, round, and connected. You can't ask for more than that. Whenever you hear a bass player that you like, what it really boils down to will be the tone or choice of notes that you really like - or maybe it's both. Take a minute to think about how many bass players that you know from back in the days of J that tried to sound just like Jaco. Think about Louis Johnson, Larry Graham or Anthony Jackson. There were many clones or wannabes. I am not saying that this is a bad thing or a good thing - it is just a thing that is what it is. When I listen to a bass player, sometimes it's the tone. Sometimes it's the choice of notes or maybe the speed and accuracy that this player has. Let me give you a better idea of how I relate to hearing a bassist. When I hear Marcus Miller, the first thing I recognize is his tone. When I hear Stanley Clarke, the first thing that tells me it's Stanley is his tone and choice of notes. When I hear Victor Bailey, I recognize his tone, choice of notes and at times speed and accuracy. When I listen to Damian Erskine, I recognize his tone and choice of notes. When I hear Jaco, it's his tone, choice of notes and accuracy playing fretless. To be able to notice these things are all a part of Bass-ick theory.

Concentrate on your own sound so that it's pleasant and enjoyable to the ear. Even though it is personal how you arrive at attaining your tone, it should always be pleasant to the ear. I was very fortunate to grow up in an environment where I was surrounded with bass players. Most were older and more experienced. I had the opportunity to listen to guys like **Tony Bunn, Gary Grainger, Mark Russell, Ernest Abdul-Raheem, Skeet, Vince Loving**. All these guys are great players, and they all have their own distinct tone. So, I felt that the least I could do was to work on my tone. It took years until I finally arrived at the satisfaction of my own sound/tone. Another one of my favorite bassists and a great friend is Latin bassist **Tony Banda.** Tony has a great tone. Check him out on many of the records by Poncho Sanchez, or the Banda Bros. records. The combination of a great tone and a good groove can go a long way.

No matter what style you choose, your tone will be important. I remember in 1981, I brought a Yellow jackets album. It had an insect – a bumble bee or some kind of bug that could sting you - on the front cover. I listened to it so much that I had to buy a second copy. What attracted me most was the tone and how fluid the bass player was. I have purchased every album they produced since that day. **Jimmy Haslip** is one of my favorite bassists. I would bet that if he only played three notes, I would recognize his tone. Sometimes a good way to check out the tone of a bassist is by going to a small venue where you can hear everything better. Maybe get there early so you can see what he or she is using. If he or she is approachable, ask questions. A personal goal that I like to reach is to have at least one person on every gig to mention either verbally or non-verbally that they enjoyed or dug the bass tone. Whenever I play an **AZOLA BASS** I don't have to work too hard because Azola basses do most of the work for you. Steve is a great bass builder. His work speaks for itself, and his instruments are played by many bassists scattered throughout the world. This isn't a plug for Steve (yes, it is), because he's retired. But maybe if we punch him, he might come out of retirement and build basses again.

I compiled a list of twenty-five bass players. The list is broken into two sections. The section on the left consists of bassists that play acoustic and or electric. The section on the right is compiled of bassists that I have heard play electric bass. Take a look at the list and check off how many you can Identify by their tone. For me, I can score 25/25 on a good day for the bassists listed. Take a shot at it, or start creating your own list. You will probably be pleasantly surprised at how many you can recognize.

Milt Hinton	James Jamerson
Ray Brown	Anthony Jackson
Jimmy Blanton	Jimmy Haslip
Oscar Pettiford	Maximo Rodriguez
Ron Carter	Marcus Miller
Slam Stewart	Gary Grainger
Eddie Gomez	Jaco Pastorius
Scott Lafaro	Victor Bailey
Dave Holland	Victor Wooton
Stanley Clarke A/E	Louis Johnson
John Patitucci A/E	Larry Graham
Ruben Rodriguez A/E	
Rene Camacho A/E	_____
Tony Banda A/E	

Any takers on the 25/25 challenge ??????

Any bassist mentioned throughout Bass-ick theory continues to be a very strong A) positive mentor, B) role model, C) friend or selection D) ALL Of The ABOVE to me.

"Don't Be a problem on stage,
  Don't be a problem off stage."
                    Rodney "Skeet" Curtis

"When the bandleader is wrong, he's right."
                              -Bill Dotts

Attitude and Vibe

Be happy about what you do. I believe music is a very spiritual way to communicate with others. To me, the bass has a very strong ability to move people. We all are affected by sounds that we hear one way or another. I like to keep things moving in a positive way with just about everything I do. When I am listening to music live or on video, I also watch the musicians' body language. I watched a very nice documentary of Chick Corea and he mentioned that he prefers the musicians in the band to look at each other when playing, because they are playing to and for each other. I really like that idea. Have you had the pleasant experience of watching the Grainger brothers perform? They both smile when they play, even during a ridiculously difficult section of the music. When you smile, it adds positive energy to the music. Smiling also makes our world a better place. When you are on a gig, realize that you are sharing the gift of music. If you are a guest or asked to sub for a fellow bassist, be a good sub. Be a good addition to the unit. When we play, we share. When you are up on the band stand doing your thing, you are sharing your energy. Your presence and music are sending a message. The message you are sending might not be what you were intending to send, but it is what is. I remember years ago I saw one national recording artist and he had a special guest with him. The special guest was set up on the far opposite end of the stage, far away from the rest of the band. He stayed there the entire performance. I spent most of the night trying to figure out what that was all about. When I think about the live performances that I have enjoyed the most it was where you could see and feel the musicians were having fun and enjoying what they were doing. We had a music venue called Painter's Mills. They had a small stage that slowly revolved during the entire concert. The revolving stage made every act that performed there a very intimate listening situation. When it comes to hearing a group perform live, there are several that I really enjoy but there are two in particular, but I won't mention any names (Poncho Sanchez, Yellow jackets) but when I hear them I want to listen to every note. I want to hear the last beat and note of the last song.

"Never allow yourself to slip into complacency, or any situation that allows your dreams to wait until tomorrow."
                                            -Eddie Resto

I hang out a little bit after the last song to see if they are going to play another tune. I am sure we all have groups that we really enjoy the same way.

Exercise # 8 Practice playing your bass from the 12th fret and higher - don't go below the 12th fret. Most of us get comfortable playing everything in the lower area of the bass. Learn a tune to play but stay in the area of the 12th fret and higher.

Exercise # 9 Change the overall tone of your bass to a completely different tone. Most of us will decide how and what to play according to the tone we have.

Exercise # 10 Imagine that you are NOT playing a bass. Imagine you are playing another instrument such as a saxophone, flute or violin. This will allow new ideas of phrasing to enter into your mind. This might also cause you to use bigger notes, shorter notes, quick, loud, fast, soft, or repeated notes. These little things will allow you to become more creative. The more creative you become, the easier it will be for you to relax and create enjoyable music on the gig.

Practice

Milt used to say to me, "Tony, don't start out practicing things you already know." He would say that if you pick up your bass and play something that you already know how to play, as soon as you finish playing you should reach into your pocket and take out a quarter. Put the quarter into your opposite hand, then place the quarter into your other pocket. He said you have just entertained yourself and you might as well be paid for

"Always play with passion and honesty and you will always be in demand."
　　　　　　　　　　　　　　　　　　－Larry Kimpel

entertaining yourself. He would follow that up by saying, "Before you pick up your bass, think about and decide what you are going to attempt. Once you have decided, make an effort to do it." He would go on to say that even if you don't succeed in doing that task to the fullest, you have gotten a little bit better. And who knows? Maybe next time you will arrive at your predicted level of achievement. I know some of us entertain ourselves for hours on end. Add up the quarters when you are done and pay yourself. Even better, develop your personal practice routine. I will share my personal practice routine, and then we can take a look at a small glimpse of another routine.

When I decide to practice, I make a list of things I want to work on. Somewhere I got the idea to use an hour glass. I searched online for hour glasses. I found several, but one in particular stood out to me. This hour glass is made of a beautiful cherry wood, deep reddish in color, and it is filled with purple sand. This has absolutely nothing to do with practice, but I decided to purchase this one, which was set up for 60 minutes. As usual, I went overboard. I bought the 60 minute, 45 minute, 30 minute, 15 minute, 5 minute and the 3 minute hour glasses. I found a way to use them all. I might use the 3 minute hour glass to force myself to figure out a rhythm or accent. Maybe the 30 minute one to read a portion of a saxophone melody. Plenty of times I stumble on something that is very challenging and I give myself 30-45 minutes to figure it out. If I decide to do an eight hour practice it would look something like this:

One hour – sight reading
One hour - walking bass lines over chord changes
One hour - playing scales
One hour - playing chords and arpeggios & inversions
One hour - working on learning a new melody
One hour - working on solos
One hour - learning a new song
One hour - studying theory or trying to dissect a new tune

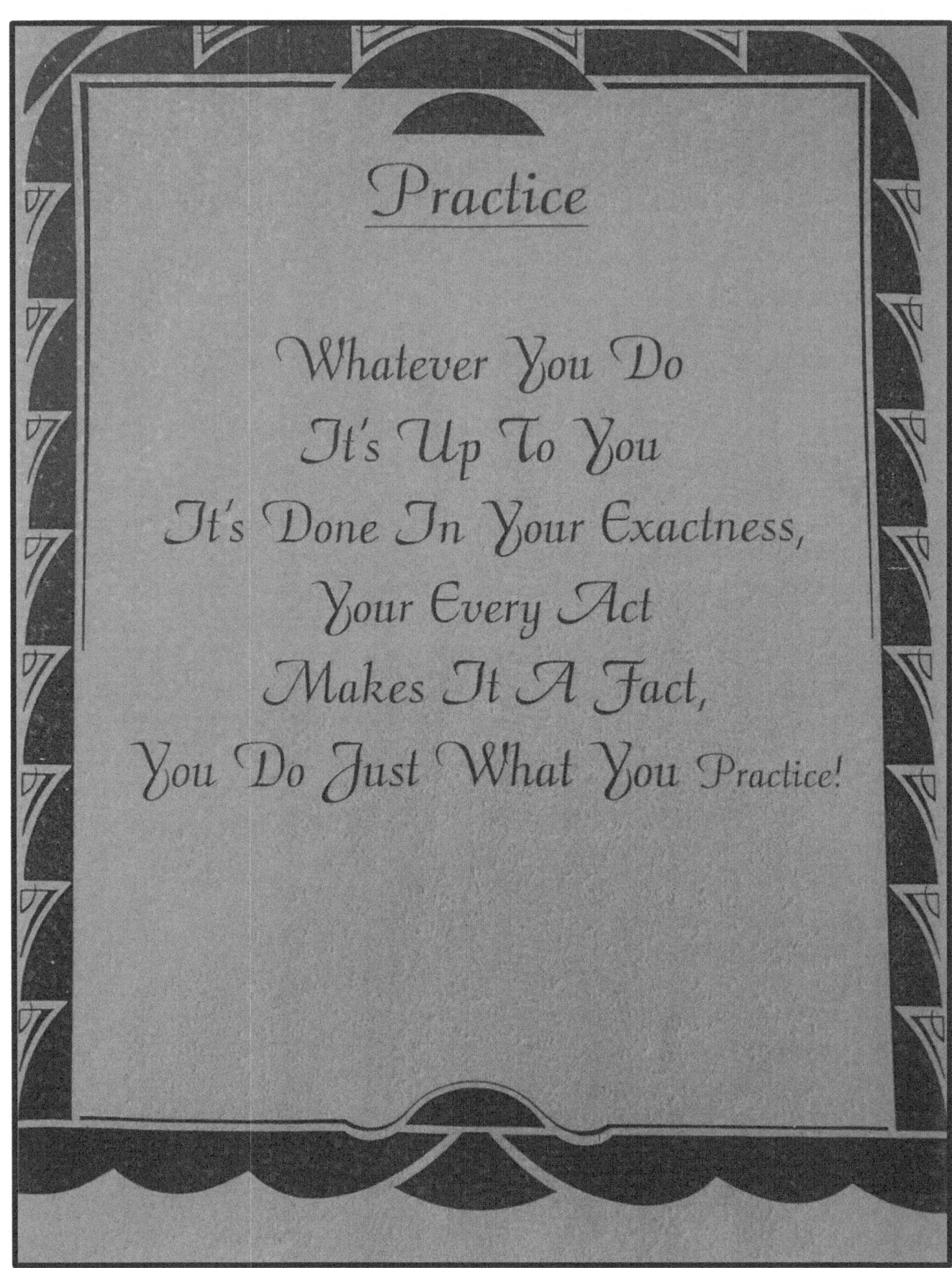

Practice

Whatever You Do
It's Up To You
It's Done In Your Exactness,
Your Every Act
Makes It A Fact,
You Do Just What You Practice!

I don't do the whole straight 8-hour practice. I break it up into sections. I might do two hours straight and then eat a meal or take a break. I might chill out and watch TV. Then go back for another couple of hours. I might even take a short nap, but I get the whole 8 hours completed and check off everything on the list before the day is over. This is very doable. It can also be broken down into eight, 30 minute sections. This might seem like a bit much but it's not. In 1993, while I was stopped at a red light, I saw a man that I thought was handing out some type of flyer. As I got closer, I observed that he was selling something. I motioned for him to come to my vehicle. I could see that he was sort of hesitant to come closer, because at the time I was on duty in a marked Maryland State Police patrol vehicle. Once he got closer, I saw what he was selling. He was asking only one dollar, but I gave him five instead. I still have the item he sold me. I keep it in my practice room. You can see it on the left.

"It's not considered trespassing when you cross your own musical boundaries."
—Marcus Boganey

Learning new tunes

I am sure most of you have heard of bassist Damian Erskine. If not, check him out asap. First of all, let me say this he is a fantastic bassist, musician, and overall wonderful human being. Check this out. When Damian approaches a tune to practice, he will look at each chord of the tune. Ok, what's different about that? Nothing yet. But next he arpeggiates each chord in time through the whole tune. Then he will arpeggiate each chord in the first inversion in time. Then go back and arpeggiate each chord in the second inversion in time. then go back again and arpeggiate the chord in the third inversion in time. That's putting in some serious work. I can only imagine the melodic ideas that enter into his head after this. In my honest opinion I believe that bass players like **Damian Erskine, Anthony Jackson, Jimmy Haslip** and a few others are highly intellectual, spiritual beings, I'm just saying. It is impossible to play the way they play without being in touch with some things on another level. I also believe that we all can head towards a higher direction by altering our approaches to the blessings that we were given as musicians.

Exercise # 11 Find a piece of sheet music of any style, any clef. See if you can identify the intervals you see. Try singing the intervals. Try playing whatever you see.

Exercise # 12 Practice your Major, minor and any other scales using only one string, Then, try using only two strings.

Exercise # 13 Whichever program you use to practice, try to loop one or two chords and experiment playing non chord notes against the chord. Take note of any non-chord tone that sounds good and add it to your memory of sounds. Find out what the flat nine, sharp nine and others sound like.

"You know, sometimes I don't say anything to Leroy when he makes quotes. I just look at him, nod my head and say, 'Ok!'"
—Tony Muhammad

The more you work on understanding the chords and how they relate to each other, the easier it will be for you to get through the tunes. I remember in the early 80's I was on a gig in Washington, D.C. with a really good saxophonist and piano player. The music was sounding really beautiful that gig. I don't think I can remember the names of the sax player or the pianist since it's been so many years ago (Stewart Dailey, Liz Beckman). During the break between sets, the sax and pianist said to me, "Tony it would be a good idea if you could play a mixture of chords and melody of a tune as a solo piece." I said, "Yes, that's a great idea. I'll work on that." Then ten minutes later the pianist said, "Con Alma is a good tune to work on." I said, "Ok, thanks." At this point I was still not getting the whole point. Then about two minutes before hit time, she said, "Right now." I said, "Right now what?" She said, "We are not going back on stage until after your solo piece." As I mentioned earlier, there are no curse words in this book, but I can type in #@~*^#. If you know me, you have a good idea of how I operate. I had no idea how it was going to turn out, but it went really well. While I was playing, I glanced over to the sax and piano player and they were smiling. It might not be a bad idea to chalk up this unexpected on-the-spot learning experience that happened to me as a way to improve your bass playing.

Throughout my entire life my friends and I have always shared our experiences as a way to help each other learn from the issues in life that we encountered. I hope that anything that you pick up from **Bass-ick Theory** will inspire you to take the next step in becoming better at what we all love to do. If not anything else, you can laugh at the crazy stuff that has happened to me. There was another gig in Washington, DC. What is it about DC that gets me into trouble? Anyway, I was a member of the DC Musicians Union and we were doing green sheet gigs during the summer. We all had our individual gigs, so we decided to share our gigs with the same crew. One day we needed a drummer and we called to get a replacement drummer. She was a great jazz drummer. After the gig, she mentioned that she enjoyed my

"OK, OK, I got my part, but I just don't know what it is."
— Leroy

"What you gonna do now???"

playing and asked if I could join her with a month's worth of gigs at a club called Twin's. I said sure. She set up a rehearsal at her place. We all arrived at the same time. She put the music on the stands and rehearsal began. The first tune was a standard tune. I played without a problem, because the chords were right in front of me. The next tune was an original composition that she had written. There were no chords on the chart. I tried to fake it. She stopped the music and counted the tune off again. The second time she stopped playing and said to me, "Tony, can you play what's on the chart please?" I took another stab at it. This time she got up from behind the drums, walked over to me and said, "Give me your bass." I gave it to her, and she played what was written on the chart. While she was playing, she said "This is what I wrote." I made it through the rest of the rehearsal but asked if I could take the charts home to study them. Immediately when I got home, I worked on the charts and got the music down. It took a few situations like this before I got my act together. I am sure we all have stories that we can share that are similar to this. I would hope that we share them with others in order to help others see the bigger picture.

I remember going on a gig with a fellow bassist and good friend of mine, **Mark Russell**. I asked Mark what tunes he was going to play on the gig. I don't remember if he answered or what he may have said, but when we arrived, I found out that he was not aware of the tunes that he was going to play on the gig. I met the musical director, who had some very large charts. That was the first time I had seen the entire music score paper, it was very large. The director placed the music on a stand where both he and Mark could see. What happened after that I will never forget. They ran over more than twenty different tunes, just playing a snippet of this and that. They went from tune to tune in a matter of minutes. They exchanged jokes and were both completely comfortable during the process. After going over the tunes in a matter of minutes, they stopped and just chilled out until the down beat. That was the deciding factor for me. I was sold on getting to the next level.

"Hey Mo, you asked what I thought about Bass players, well here you go:
Some of the bass players have been very easy going and some of them should have been comedians. Some use the slap technique or play with their thumbs which make them percussionist. Then you have someone like Mr. Anthony Jackson who stayed away from slap bass playing. One thing about Anthony is that he can hear things before you get there. There are other guys that have the same quality in their playing also. But just having the ability to sit and play music and listen to the overall picture is unique. That's the first thing I learned about Anthony is that you just cannot listen to yourself! I'm not saying that all the other bass players I have played with don't have these qualities, but they display it in different ways. The other thing I love about bass players is that a bass player should have great timing and great imagination. If you ever give me a bass player to work with that's unmusical, has bad timing, no imagination and no sense of humor we're going to have problems! Dennis Out!"

—Dennis Chambers

"Hear what you play,
    play what you hear."
—Anonymous

Exercise # 14 Listening Exercise – Within a few minutes, most of us while listening to music have already picked out what the bass player is doing. Take time to isolate each instrument independently and follow that instrument until the tune ends. After that, start again and choose a different instrument. This will strengthen your awareness of what's going on in the tune. It will also help you in playing your bass line because you will really see how the parts are synced together.

It may not seem like such a big idea, but it is rather important that the area where you practice or play your bass should be designated as that. If possible, create a space to practice. The less you have in this area that is not related to music, the better. This may not always be possible, but give it your best effort.

I truly believe that being kind is one of the best things we can all profit from in all situations in life. As we are kind to each other, we send out signals that are returned. Sometimes just by being kind we can change the energy from not so pleasant to kind. There's an interesting video that you should check out on YouTube - it's called "Everything is a Signal." Listen to it carefully and remember above all that the message is what is most important. Also, another video to watch would be saxophonist Joe Lovano's master class on improvisation. Joe is one of my favorite musicians. You will feel his positive energy coming through with every note he plays and every word he says. I can also feel his peaceful spirit coming thru every note he plays. This and lots of other things are all a part of **BASS-ICK THEORY**. It is far more than just picking up a bass and playing some riffs. When you play, take the time to watch and feel the responses from your audience. If a particular tune goes over well, think about whether you need to extend it or play another similar one shortly after. It may also be a good idea to center yourself mentally prior to the downbeat. Jazz pianist Kenny Werner has a great book called

"Effortless Mastery," where he goes into detail about putting yourself into the zone.

Most of us end up owning several basses, because we just can't help ourselves. Might be a good idea to take the time to understand what makes each bass different. We should know other than looks why we prefer one bass over another. We should know which basses have the right tone for the gig. When you have a minute, try selecting a bass that would not be your first or second option for a gig/tune. Play that bass anyway. The difference in the bass will cause you to play differently than you normally would play. We play and feel what we play according to how we hear it. Remember Jaco said his sound was in his hands. I believe that he could have picked up any bass and it would have sounded great, and we all would recognize it was his sound. Try picking up a fretless bass. Play a melody and keep an eye on your intonation. Don't sacrifice the integrity of the melody. If your intonation is off, don't try to cover it up with a slur or slide. Get it right, take your time.

Exercise # 15 "And I hope you've got your colored pencils"

When I was in school studying music theory, we were blessed to have a wonderful professor. He was a very interesting person. He had a distinct voice and always made jokes. Every time we were about to analyze a new tune, He would always say, "I hope you brought your colored pencils." The class would laugh, and I never really understood what was so funny. One day I stayed after class, waited until everyone left, and asked him why he always said that. I'm glad I did. What he meant was to use colored pencils to indicate the chords that are from the same key signature. He started out by designating one specific color for all of the dominant chords in the song with the same color. The next thing he did was look to the left of the dominant chord to see what chord it was. If it was a minor chord, then most likely it was a two chord from the same key as the dominant chord. If so, he would color the two chord and the top of the dominant chord the same color. Then he would look to the right of the dominant chord to see if there was a Major chord. If so, it was most likely the tonic chord / one chord (a 2-5-1 progression). He would continue throughout the tune using different colors when there was a different key signature. If he ran into a key signature that he had already seen he would reuse the same color for that key. By the time he went through the whole tune, you could see the pattern. This was very clear to me after seeing it. He mentioned that this would help me realize when the tune was moving to a new tonal center, which in turn would give me the opportunity to create a more stable bass line or take a better solo. Give this a shot, I'm sure it will help you. **Get your colored pencils.**

Sharing and teaching

I Like to think there is a slight difference between sharing and teaching. Normally, when we teach, we show or tell. When you show or tell something, is it the absolute truth? I really don't think so, because there are many ways to do things and all things change. When you share, you give. It could be advice, it could be an object, etc. Let me say that again - when you share, you give. When you are sharing ideas or suggestions related to music, you are sharing what you have experienced along with why it did or did not work. Sharing is very powerful when it comes to music. When you watch a performance live or even a video, the artist is sharing his or her expressions and feelings via the music. When you sit down during a lesson, I think you are sharing your thoughts as to how you handle certain musical situations. The person might decide to take your advice verbatim. But since there are always several ways to accomplish any musical task, that should be a given. A big part of **BASS-ICK THEORY** is to share. Some are hesitant to share for many reasons. Milt always taught me to share what I know, just as he shared with me. He also said that the only way you can show that you know something is to share it with someone and have them reiterate it back to you - that would be your proof. Sharing is not done by talking alone, it is also done by how you live your life. **Your life is your message.** When you see or hear music that moves your spirit, that energy comes from a source that moved the creator of the music very similar to how it moved you. Depending on how an artist is feeling at a given moment, they may play a tune with a different feel all together. The feel could change every night. When Chick Corea asked the members of the band to look at each other when they play, there was a reason for that. Those guys enjoy playing with each other and enjoy being in each other's company. That reflects in the music. There's a combination of many things you see when you watch a performance. At the moment, you are receiving the total package each musician is presenting to you at that time. Whether you want it to be true or not, every time you play, that is the best that you can do at that given moment. I remember going to the NAMM one year and I stumbled onto a booth where a bass player was just about to start his clinic. There were only two chairs left and my friend and I sat in those two seats. Within minutes the clinic began. I did not know that the two seats we were in were meant for participants of the clinic. The next thing I knew, I had a bass in my hand, and I was asked to play a bass line. He said, "Play anything, any line that you can think of." I played a downward bass line of about five or six notes. Then he said transpose that line to another key. So, without thinking, I played the line in the key that he requested, and one or two notes were wrong by a half step. He immediately stopped me and said, "I am assuming that you are not a reader." I said, "Sure, I can read very well." He then moved on to the next victim. I found out that his whole method of communicating was by first creating a situation and then correcting it. That might work for some, but that does not really work for me. After the clinic, I made a few phone calls in reference to this person and learned from extremely reliable sources that this was the regular method of operation for this person. As far as the bass line I played for him, the proper way to handle that situation would be to first check the intervals in the line you are playing before transposing it. I knew that at the time, but didn't take the time to do that. I appreciate any learning experience for whatever the outcome may be. This and anything else that comes up is a part of **BASS-ICK THEORY**. I work every single day with efforts that I hope will help me become a better human being. I am sure if you are reading this you are doing likewise. No, let me say that a different way, I know that those who are reading this are in fact doing this, because my circle is filled with very positive people. I hope that there was something that was shared in this initial volume of **BASS-ICK THEORY** that will help make you a better bassist, musician, and all around better human being. Also, I'd like to say that every single bass player that I have mentioned continues to be a positive role model and mentor to me. I would like to thank them for their contributions towards making this happen.

"Study yourself."

-Tony Muhammad

Photo of the author by Ana C.

"Am I getting paid for all this?
Can you give me cash right after the gig instead of a check, cause I gotta handle some Business."

— Leroy

Tony Muhammad was born in Baltimore and studied music at the Skidmore Jazz Institute, the Manhattan School of Music, and, most notably, with Milt Hinton. After relocating to California, he was the Music Director and leader of the house band at Anthology, a popular music venue in San Diego's Little Italy. Tony has spent forty-five years studying and playing different styles of music. His students know that he has a plan for every moment he spends with them, as he continually challenges them to learn and grow and to be the best bassists and human beings they can be.

Acknowledgements

I would like to thank the following people:

Andy Greenberg – Andy's guitar, Thousand Palms, CA

Russell Harris – Basslayerz.com, bass caps, straps and gear
Little Elm, TX

Doug Parent – bass repairs, San Diego, CA

Steve Azola – Azola Basses, San Diego, CA

Helane Fronek – editing, San Diego, CA

Made in United States
North Haven, CT
06 November 2021